GUSTAV KLIMT

25 MASTERWORKS

Fig. 1. Gustav Klimt in the garden of his Josefstädterstrasse studio, c. 1912–14

GUSTAV KLIMT

25 MASTERWORKS

JANE KALLIR

ABRADALE, NEW YORK

I would like to convey my warmest thanks to Alice Strobl for her advice in the preparation of this manuscript, and to Hildegard Bachert for her painstaking assistance.   J.K.

The following publications have served as the principal sources for the information and quotations contained herein:

Marian Bisanz-Prakken. *Gustav Klimt: Der Beethovenfries.* Salzburg: Residenz Verlag, 1977

Wolfgang Georg Fischer. *Gustav Klimt und Emilie Flöge.* Vienna: Verlag Christian Brandstätter, 1987

Salomon Grimberg. "Adele." *Art and Antiques,* summer 1986, pp. 70–75, 90

Werner Hofmann. *Gustav Klimt.* Boston: New York Graphic Society, 1977

Christian M. Nebehay. *Gustav Klimt Dokumentation.* Vienna: Verlag der Galerie Christian M. Nebehay, 1969

Fritz Novotny and Johannes Dobai. *Gustav Klimt.* Salzburg: Verlag der Galerie Welz, 1967, 2d ed. 1975

Alice Strobl. *Gustav Klimt: Die Zeichnungen.* (3 vols.) Salzburg: Verlag der Galerie Welz, 1980, 1982, 1984

All illustrations have been referenced in accordance with their listings in the catalogue raisonné by Fritz Novotny and Johannes Dobai (see above). The designation "destroyed" refers to a group of paintings, stored at the Schloss Immendorf, burned by retreating German troops during the closing days of World War II.

Project Director: Margaret L. Kaplan

Editor: Johanna Awdry

Designer: Doris Leath

The publishers gratefully acknowledge the assistance of Verlag Galerie Welz, Salzburg, in supplying the color photographic material used in this book.

ISBN 978-1-4351-2455-4

Copyright © 1989 Galerie St Etienne, New York

Published in 1995 by Abrams, an imprint of ABRAMS.

This 2010 edition published for Barnes & Noble, Inc., by arrangement with ABRAMS.

Printed and bound in China
10 9 8 7 6 5 4 3 2 1

THE ART OF BOOKS SINCE 1949

115 West 18th Street
New York, NY 10011
www.abramsbooks.com

Given the Klimt family's financial straits, all hopes were pinned on the success of Gustav and his two younger brothers, Ernst and Georg. After eight years of primary school (*Bürgerschule*), Gustav received a scholarship to the Kunstgewerbeschule (School of Applied Arts), which had been founded in 1867 on the model of England's South Kensington School and Museum (forerunner of today's Victoria and Albert Museum) in order to improve the status and international stature of Austrian crafts. The Kunstgewerbeschule was essentially a trade school, and Gustav's logical options were either to enter industry or to teach. However, during this period Vienna was experiencing a phenomenal building boom centered on the broad circular boulevard, the Ringstrasse, that had recently replaced the ancient ramparts surrounding the inner city. The Ringstrasse boom had created a wonderful market for painters, who were lured by the dozens to decorate the new public structures and private palaces, conceived in pseudo-historical styles (Gothic for the city hall, Neoclassical for the parliament) that lent an air of pompous artificiality to the entire era. At one end of the professional spectrum was Hans Makart, who got the choicest commissions and set all Vienna awhirl with his sensuous but decorous nudes and adjunct crazes such as "Makart hats" and "Makart bouquets" (arrangements of dried flowers and feathers). At or near the other end of the spectrum was Gustav Klimt's teacher Ferdinand Laufberger, whose contributions to the Ringstrasse are today all but forgotten, though at the time they kept his Kunstgewerbeschule workshop buzzing.

Fig. 3. *Art of Ancient Greece I (Athena with Nike)*. 1890–91. Oil on stucco, 90 1/2 × 90 1/2" (230 × 230 cm.). Spandrel in the Kunsthistorisches Museum, Vienna (N/D 48)

It did not take Laufberger long to recognize that Gustav Klimt, the most talented of his students, and his brother Ernst, who had entered the Kunstgewerbeschule in 1878, had a future as decorative muralists. They and their classmate Franz Matsch were invited to contribute to Laufberger's commissions, and by 1880 they had begun to receive assignments in their own right. The *Künstlerkompagnie* (Artists' Company) of Matsch and the two Klimt brothers was formulated along the medieval workshop principle espoused by Laufberger, and the individual hands of the contributors can scarcely be discerned in their early work. In 1883, the trio opened their own studio, and for the next few years they spent much of their time traveling around the Austrian empire painting curtains and murals for provincial theaters. Sensing that the Ringstrasse boom could not last forever, the group longed to work in the capital, and finally, in 1886, they received one of their first major commissions: the staircase decorations for Vienna's new Burgtheater. As a sideline, they were also asked to create a pictorial record of the old Burgtheater before it was torn down, an assignment that blossomed into a sort of who's who of Viennese society, rendered with photographic fidelity in Klimt's large gouache of the auditorium (fig. 2). The staircase frescoes and the gouache earned the artist his first serious accolades: he received the Gold Service Cross from the Emperor Franz Josef for the former in 1888, and the Emperor's Prize for the latter in 1890. Already, in 1887, Klimt had been hailed as Makart's logical successor, and this position seemed confirmed when, in 1890, the *Künstlerkompagnie* was given the older artist's final decorative commission, left unfinished at his death in 1884: the spandrels for the staircase of the Kunsthistorisches Museum (Art History Museum). The company's previous work, a virtual encyclopedia of historical theatrical imagery, had prepared them well for this assignment, which required detailed study of period costumes and works from the museum's collection. Klimt's taste for iconographical borrowing, honed during this formative period, was to remain with him all his life. To the Kunsthistorisches Museum spandrels he added another element that was to become a hallmark of his later style: the development of a prototypical female beauty, a very contemporary persona whose vibrant immediacy belied the historical accuracy of her costume (fig. 3). Here, for the first time, Klimt's approach was immediately distinguishable from that of his partners.

Fig. 4. *Love*. 1895. Oil on canvas, 23 5/8 × 17 3/8" (60 × 44 cm.). Wien Museum (N/D 68)

In 1892, celebrating over a decade of successful collaboration, the *Künstlerkompagnie* moved to a new studio on the Josefstädterstrasse. It was, as it turned out, one of the last moves the group would make together. That summer, Klimt's father was felled by a stroke (instilling in the artist a lifelong fear of succumbing to a similar fate), and in December his brother Ernst died of pericarditis. These events left Klimt deeply shaken and triggered an artistic withdrawal that lasted some five years. During the period between 1892 and 1897, the number of public

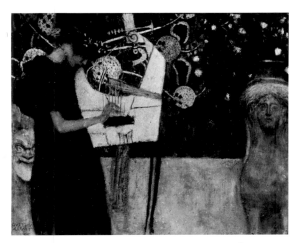

Fig. 5. *Music I.* 1895. Oil on canvas, 14⅝ × 17½″ (37 × 44.5 cm.). Neue Pinakothek, Munich (N/D 69)

Fig. 6. *Schubert at the Piano.* 1899. Oil on canvas, 59 × 78¾″ (150 × 200 cm.). Destroyed (N/D 101)

Fig. 7. Poster for the First Secession Exhibition. 1898

commissions undertaken by him dwindled to almost nothing, and his collaboration with Matsch effectively ceased. At one point Matsch discreetly vacated the Josefstädterstrasse premises, which Klimt would occupy by himself until 1914, when he moved to his final studio in Vienna's Hietzing district. It was Matsch alone who, in 1892, received the next significant commission to come their way: the ceiling paintings for the auditorium at the University of Vienna. However, when, in 1893, Matsch's preliminary sketches were rejected by the Ministry of Culture and Education, Klimt's participation was solicited. This last, disastrous collaboration between the one-time partners was, as it transpired, to prove a turning point in Klimt's evolving career, for by the time his three University canvases were finished, he had left Matsch's conventional world far behind. Influenced by foreign symbolists such as Jan Toorop, Ferdinand Khnopff, and Ferdinand Hodler, Klimt had developed a far more personal approach to allegory that categorically rejected the rote historicism of the Makart era (figs. 4, 5).

As Klimt's art became more idiosyncratic, more removed from the public arena of the Ringstrasse, his lifestyle itself became more remote, his thought processes unfathomable. He was not exactly a hermit: according to a set routine, he had his breakfast (including a large portion of whipped cream) every morning at the same café, where colleagues were always welcome to join him with the proviso that they refrain from talking about art. From here he went to his studio, where he worked until evening with nothing but a plate of fruit for sustenance and a bevy of models (retained regardless of whether they were needed) for companionship. Cats played freely among the drawings that littered the floor, sometimes multiplying to the point where friends surreptitiously removed a few in order to reduce the population. At night, Klimt frequented artists' taverns or went home to supper with his mother and sisters, eating in silence and then going directly to bed. He was not a man of many words, either spoken or written. He did not like to answer letters, and when the accumulated correspondence had reached a certain mass, it (like the cats) was simply removed. Despite his multitudinous social and professional contacts, only the sketchiest accounts of his personality have been preserved. Bearlike in both strength and appearance, the rotund, bearded artist was, according to one acquaintance, thoroughly "animalistic": he even smelled like an animal. Tanned like a sailor, according to another, he was an enthusiastic athlete, whose interests included wrestling, bowling, and rowing; he took long walks almost daily. His closest companion was Emilie Flöge (plate 5), with whom he spent almost every summer on the Attersee, yet even today it is not known whether they were merely good friends or, as has often been maintained, lovers. As to Klimt's other relationships with women—the society beauties who posed for him, and the poor unfortunates who bore his illegitimate children (some fourteen of whom made claims on his estate)—all that survives is a scattering of facts and a huge amount of innuendo. Klimt once advised those who wanted to know about him to look at his art, and indeed the obsessive love of privacy with which he shrouded his life has left us little choice.

An unlikely rebel, the good-natured Klimt nonetheless grew increasingly alienated from the conventional forces that dominated Viennese art circles. In this he was not alone, for many of the younger artists felt that the Künstlerhaus (Artists' House)—the sole local outlet for the promotion of contemporary art—was unfairly biased in favor of its older, more established members and too set in its ways to maintain adequate contact with foreign developments. After a few discouraging attempts at reform, the progressive minority, led by Klimt, decided to secede from the Künstlerhaus. The Secession's founding, in 1897, could hardly have come at a more propitious moment. The boom period that had brought the Ringstrasse to completion and Makart to glory had also created a new class of self-made millionaires, would-be aristocrats who, lacking the imprimatur of hereditary nobility, sought to buy into culture through a wholehearted support of the arts. Within a few months of its founding, the Secession had attracted a sizable financial contribution from the industrialist Karl Wittgenstein (whose daughter would later be painted by Klimt, plate 8) and persuaded the City of Vienna to donate land for a new building. By the end of 1898, the building was complete, and with its successful

second exhibition (the first had taken place the previous spring in rented quarters), the Secession was almost instantly established as a force to be reckoned with.

The Secessionists, united in their opposition to the status quo, formulated a far-reaching program of exhibitions and publications designed to shake the Viennese out of their complacency. Early Secession images were intended to be provocative, and they did not fail. Klimt's poster for the opening exhibition in 1898, boldly depicting a young Theseus in symbolic battle with a retrograde Minotaur (fig. 7), was censored for its exposed genitalia, while his painting of *Pallas Athena* (plate 2) raised a small tempest of controversy. However, these episodes were relatively innocuous compared to the scandal that greeted his first painting for the University of Vienna, *Philosophy* (fig. 8), when it was exhibited at the Secession in 1900. In order to understand the campaign that was subsequently waged against Klimt, it is necessary to momentarily resurrect the body of knowledge—entailing classical Greek and Latin—and its attendant imagery, comprising generally understood mythological, historical, and biblical themes, that served as common ground for allegorical painting in the nineteenth century. Today's public, having largely jettisoned such arcane studies, has a far more fluid approach to metaphor than did Klimt's peers, to whom the idea of presenting *Philosophy* in a universalized, non-historical setting was anathema. It is significant that some of the most vocal critics of *Philosophy* and the second University painting, *Medicine* (first exhibited in 1901)—professors who after all knew better than anyone what these disciplines were all about—repeatedly complained that the paintings had nothing to do with their purported themes. These learned gentlemen simply could not recognize a subject not cloaked in the conventional iconography, despite the fact that each of the paintings addressed its particular topic quite directly. For this reason, ironically, few grasped the one aspect of the paintings that was truly shocking: for if there was a secret message hidden in Klimt's tangle of bodies—the newborn infants, embracing lovers, despairing elderly, the ill and dying, the dead—it is that man is born to suffer and die, and human attempts to intervene—philosophy and medicine—are of no avail. Even less conciliatory is the last University canvas, *Jurisprudence* (fig. 10), painted when Klimt was already bombarded with assaults on the first two pictures and exhibited for the first time in 1903. Departing from the compositional structure of the two prior paintings, *Jurisprudence* has at its center an emaciated, pain-wracked male nude—the criminal—ensnared in the tentacles of an octopuslike creature that might better be named "Injustice." Even if one prefers to interpret the octopus as the criminal's guilty conscience, as did the contemporary critic Ludwig Hevesi, it is

Fig. 8. *Philosophy*. 1899–1907. Oil on canvas, 169¼ × 118⅛″ (430 × 300 cm.). Destroyed (N/D 105)

Fig. 9. *Medicine*. 1900–1907. Oil on canvas, 169¼ × 118⅛″ (430 × 300 cm.). Destroyed (N/D 112)

Fig. 10. *Jurisprudence*. 1903–1907. Oil on canvas, 169¼ × 118⅛″ (430 × 300 cm.). Destroyed (N/D 128)

Fig. 11. The Beethoven Frieze: *The Hostile Forces*. 1901–1902. Casein on stucco, height 86⅝″ (220 cm.). The Secession, Vienna (N/D 127)

Fig. 12. The Beethoven Frieze: *The Chorus of Angels/A Kiss for the Entire World*. 1901–1902. Casein on stucco, height 86⅝″ (220 cm.). The Secession, Vienna (N/D 127)

Fig. 13. Cartoon for the Stoclet Frieze: *Expectation*. c. 1908–1910. Mixed media on paper, 76×45¼″ (193×115 cm.). Österreichisches Museum für angewandte Kunst, Vienna (N/D 152-B)

Fig. 14. The Stoclet Dining Room. c. 1910–11. Mosaic. Palais Stoclet, Brussels (N/D 153)

clear that the rule of law—represented by three very tiny figures in the distant background—is here as nothing compared to the barbaric forces that determine man's fate.

The controversy surrounding the University paintings—which haunted Klimt for five years, flaring up whenever he exhibited one of the three works—effectively terminated his career as a public muralist. Nonetheless, the desire to combine art and architecture lived on in the concept of the *Gesamtkunstwerk* (total artwork), which, as formulated by the Secessionists, represented the highest level of artistic brotherhood and collaboration, a fine-tuned merging of talents in pursuit of a whole greater than the sum of the parts. This idealistic aim was most successfully realized in the Secession's 1902 Beethoven Exhibition, a tribute to the composer that united Max Klinger's well-known statue, Klimt's specially commissioned Beethoven Frieze (figs. 11, 12), and paintings by lesser Secessionists in a customized setting by the architect Josef Hoffmann. The Beethoven Exhibition was widely acknowledged as an aesthetic triumph, but over the long haul the *Gesamtkunstwerk* proved better suited to the rather more mundane world of interior decoration. Seeking to bring their ideas of enlightened environmental design into the homes of the Secession's well-to-do patrons, Hoffmann and the artist Koloman Moser in 1903 founded a separate organization, the Wiener Werkstätte. The conventional easel painters within the Secession resented this development, for they felt that the Wiener Werkstätte gave an unfair financial advantage to Klimt and the other artists associated with it. A succession of minor incidents brought to a head the conflict between the two divergent factions, and in 1905 the *Klimtgruppe* quit the Secession, more or less abandoning their ambitious exhibition program together with the building that had made it possible. That same year, Klimt finally renounced the University commission and, with the help of the collector August Lederer (see plate 21), bought back his three canvases from the Ministry of Culture and Education. In one fell swoop he was forced to relinquish both the old world of official patronage and the new world of artistic brotherhood that had replaced it. It was perhaps the saddest aspect of his life that, to the end of his days, he retained an abiding faith in both.

With the Secession split, Klimt's retreat into the private sphere—to some extent ordained already when he broke with Matsch—was complete. He had long ago accuired a coterie of affluent patrons who assured his economic well-being. By the standard of his forebears, Klimt was rich; his average fee for a portrait was 20,000–30,000 kronen, roughly ten times the annual income of a working-class family. His mother and sisters, whom he supported, had no need to fall back on the earnings of brother Georg, a goldsmith like his father. Success brought Klimt into contact with surroundings very different from those of his boyhood. Alma Mahler (widow of the composer and a legendary *femme fatale*) recalled that he was something of a stranger to elegant drawing-room society. His *Bildung* (education) could not compare with that of the upper classes, and though he made a show of erudition, supposedly quoting Petrarch and Dante while he painted, his use of heavy Viennese dialect marked him as the tradesman's son he was. It may be that his habitual shyness, and the resultant paucity of personal information about him, were really the result of a singular loneliness. The leader of an entire generation of artists, Klimt was truly at home only in his studio. It was here that, in his last years, he found the solace denied him by the outer world.

When, some three years after leaving the Secession, the *Klimtgruppe* finally mustered the forces for a comprehensive exhibition—titled simply *Kunstschau* (art show)—the effect was less that of a joyful reunion than of a post-mortem. Though Klimt was undeniably the star of the show, with sixteen of his latest works displayed in a special room, it was the Expressionist Oskar Kokoschka, exhibiting here for the first time, who represented the wave of the future. Kokoschka and the slightly younger Egon Schiele (who debuted at a second *Kunstschau* in 1909) quickly moved away from the ornamental excesses of Klimt's style, stripping off the decorative fill that had become the elder artist's trademark to expose the void that had always been implicit in his *horror vacui* (figs. 15, 16). Klimt, for his part, stepped back from a direct confrontation with the void, relinquishing the philosophical thrust of the University paintings in favor of the surface glitter epitomized by his 1908 icon, *The Kiss* (plate 13). Torn between content and form, he embraced the latter, only to find that it led him nowhere. Klimt was not able to make the great leap: to perceive form *as* content and thereby progress toward true abstraction. He was thus ultimately unable to solve the riddle of *fin-de-siècle* art, for the alternative path—content as form—would be explored not by him, but by the Expressionists. The great paradox of Klimt's career was that, while he failed to effectively link up with later modernism, he nonetheless anticipated its two principal trends: abstraction and Expressionism. That he could not, in the end, categorically choose one over the other is as much a strength as a weakness, for the resultant dualism charges his entire oeuvre with a rare and powerful tension.

On January 11, 1918, Klimt suffered the fate that, ever since his father's death in 1892, he had always feared. The stroke left him partially paralyzed but able to speak, and he seemed to be making a good recovery when, in early February, he was transferred to a special clinic to receive a waterbed treatment for his bedsores. As a result, he developed pneumonia, from which he died on February 6. All Vienna mourned the loss of a man whom, despite past misunderstandings, it now rightfully recognized as its greatest painter. The most succinct epitaph was written by Egon Schiele, the leader of the next generation:

> An artist of unbelievable perfection
> A person of rare depth
> His work a shrine

Fig. 15. *Portrait of Friederike Maria Beer.* 1916. Oil on canvas, 66¹/₈ × 51¹/₈″ (168 × 130 cm.). Private collection (N/D 196)

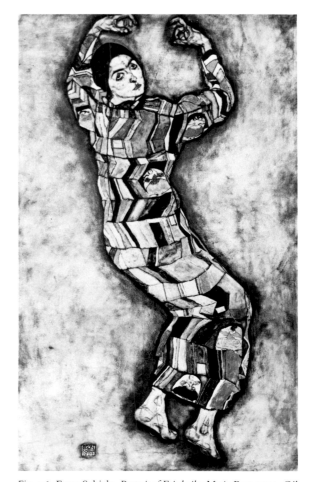

Fig. 16. Egon Schiele. *Portrait of Friederike Maria Beer.* 1914. Oil on canvas, 74³/₄ × 47³/₈″ (190 × 120.5 cm.). Private collection (Kallir 192)

PLATE I

PORTRAIT OF SONJA KNIPS

1898

Oil on canvas, 57 ¹/₈ × 57 ¹/₈″ (145 × 145 cm.)

Österreichische Galerie, Vienna

(N/D 91)

The *Portrait of Sonja Knips* was in many senses a breakthrough painting for Gustav Klimt. The period preceding it—some five years of relative inactivity—had been one of consolidation and growth, as the artist slowly weaned himself from his academic background and struggled toward his own revolutionary style. The portrait marked a firm break with the glamorous—but implicitly decadent—world of the theater, in which he had made his early name, and his first significant entry into the social stratum that fostered the rise of the Secession and later the Wiener Werkstätte. As a privately commissioned work, the painting also heralded Klimt's progressive withdrawal from the public arena of his previous activity as a muralist. It was the first in the long series of portraits depicting society ladies that was to become the mainstay of the artist's later reputation and economic well-being. Whereas formerly his work had been more or less evenly divided between male and female subjects, he was hereafter to paint women almost exclusively.

In other ways, too, the Knips portrait presaged Klimt's future development. Though the painting is not yet as fanciful or stylized as the work from the subsequent "gold" period, the musty pastels and soft, milky textures constitute a clear departure from the conventional realism of his earlier years. The influence of the American painter James McNeil Whistler is unmistakable and was remarked upon as early as 1903, though it is thought that Klimt could only have known his work from reproductions at the time. The triangular semi-profile pose and square format were to appear as recurrent compositional devices in Klimt's later portraits. A subtle competition between the subject and her inanimate surroundings—the suffocatingly high-collared dress, the striking floral arrangement—is also indicative of the sort of pictorial tension that Klimt would exploit to great effect in his mature work.

PLATE 2

PALLAS ATHENA

1898

Oil on canvas, 29 ½ × 29 ½" (75 × 75 cm.).

Wien Museum

(N/D 93)

Like the *Portrait of Sonja Knips* (plate 1), *Pallas Athena* was included in the inaugural exhibition of the Secession's building at the end of 1898, but unlike the serene portrait, which contemporary critics dubbed "the lady in pink," it became an immediate center of controversy. This controversy, foreshadowing the far greater scandal that would greet the showing of *Philosophy* (fig. 8) two years later, focused on the artist's untraditional treatment of a traditional subject, the Greek goddess of wisdom. Klimt had proved himself capable of painting a perfectly acceptable Athena some eight years earlier, when covering the spandrels of the Kunsthistorisches Museum (fig. 3), but this latest incarnation of the subject was another matter entirely. Possibly his experiences as a muralist had first prompted him to question the "reality" of conventional representational art, for in decorative commissions the concrete—yet abstract—architectural setting tends to undermine the three-dimensional illusion of the artist's painted world. It was not just family loyalty, nor his own background as the son of a goldsmith, that prompted Klimt to have his brother Georg design a special gilded frame for the 1898 *Pallas Athena,* or to echo the frame by allowing real gold to leach into the painting itself. These devices enabled him to duplicate, in miniature, the contradictions inherent in a large-scale architectural commission, giving the resultant canvas a tectonic immediacy that brought it directly into the world of the viewer.

Klimt's formal innovations generally had direct bearing on the content of his work, and the confrontational aspect of his Athena underscored a message that, if properly understood, could not help but rankle. This Athena was not just a wise woman, she was a dangerous woman. (Are not all wise women dangerous? a contemporary misogynist might have asked.) She was no longer the benign protector of the Secession seen in Klimt's poster for that organization's first exhibition (fig. 7), but an avenging warrior whose frontal stance (unlike the profile view presented in the poster) offered a direct challenge to the uncomprehending public. Like the slightly later *Nuda Veritas* (Naked Truth, fig. 17)—whose very image she holds in her hand—Athena promised exposure of cherished illusions and confrontation with unpleasant realities.

Fig. 17. *Nuda Veritas (Naked Truth).* 1899. Oil on canvas, 99¼ × 22" (252 × 56.2 cm.). Theatersammlung der Nationalbibliothek, Vienna (N/D 102)

PLATE 3

JUDITH I

1901

Oil on canvas, 33 1/8 × 16 1/2" (84 × 42 cm.)

Österreichische Galerie, Vienna

(N/D 113)

Formalistically, *Judith I* recapitulated many of the same principles already manifested in the *Pallas Athena* of 1898 (plate 2). Again, a decorative frame, designed jointly with brother Georg, tested the boundaries between illusion and reality, but Klimt went even further in allowing two-dimensional decorative elements to intrude into the body of the painting. He began to refine a vocabulary of abstract shapes—floral medallions, golden eggs and scales, undulating zigzag loops—that would, in years to come, feature ever more prominently in his work. Surprisingly, for all its radical elements, *Judith* was received far more favorably than *Pallas Athena* when, in 1901, it was shown at the Secession's tenth exhibition. By this time, of course, the scandal surrounding *Athena* had been dimmed by the horrors of the University paintings, and *Judith* was certainly tame by comparison with *Philosophy* (fig. 8) or *Medicine* (fig. 9), which premiered in the same 1901 show. Yet as one contemporary critic noted, the general acceptance of *Judith* was as illogical as the rejection of the University paintings or, several years earlier, of *Athena*. For was not Judith a woman as dangerous as Athena, if not more so? Did she not, despite her deceptively alluring dream trance, wield the severed head of Holofernes as proof of her deadly capabilities?

Iconographically, *Judith I* marks an important way station in Klimt's development of the *femme fatale,* a recurrent motif throughout his career. Unlike Athena, who seems to merge with her abstract surroundings, Judith remains very much a flesh-and-blood presence. She was, indeed, a creature of Klimt's time, as was not lost on his contemporaries. "She is one of those beautiful Jewish socialites whom one meets everywhere and who, sweeping along in their silk gowns, attract men's eyes at all the premières," noted the writer Felix Salten. "One often encounters such slender, glittering Jewish women and longs to see these decorative, flirtatious and playful creatures suddenly hurled toward a torrid destiny, to detonate the explosive power that flashes in their eyes." Klimt's artistic realization of the prevalent fantasy of sex with a dark and dangerous Jewess eloquently expressed the comingled strains of misogyny and anti-Semitism that characterized *fin-de-siècle* thought. Unlike Athena, Judith did not challenge Viennese preconceptions, but rather catered to them. The subject's sensuous abandon—suggestive of post-coital torpor—explicitly eroticizes her murderous act, playing on the then-common male fear of female sexuality. To complete the picture, one need only add that the literature of the day seriously maintained that sex was a female vice which, left unchecked, would rob man of his intellectual capabilities—which would, as Judith had, sever brain from body.

PLATE 4

ISLAND IN THE ATTERSEE

c. 1901

Oil on canvas, 39 3/8 × 39 3/8" (100 × 100 cm.)

Private collection; courtesy Galerie St. Etienne, New York

(N/D 117)

Of his three basic subject types—portraits, allegories and landscapes—Klimt came latest to landscape. Two somewhat antithetical aspects of his career seem to have been responsible for this. On the one hand, by the late 1890s he at last had the time and money to afford vacations— both literally and artistically—from the subjects that had previously provided his main economic sustenance. On the other hand, the increasingly controversial nature of his work made such vacations an emotional necessity. Initially a form of private relaxation, landscape painting eventually also became a viable source of income as the support for his more inflammatory public allegories gradually dried up.

Klimt's first landscapes can be dated to roughly 1897–98, at which time, not coincidentally, he began spending the summer months on the Attersee with the family of Emilie Flöge (plate 5). Among the group of lakes nestled in the foothills of the Alps that form the heart of the Salzkammergut region east of Salzburg, the Attersee is one of the quietest, and though it had, by Klimt's day, been an established resort for many decades, it lacked the social hubbub of such neighboring watering-holes as Ischl, where the Emperor summered. From the turn of the century until the end of his life, Klimt would, with few exceptions, spend every summer with the Flöges on this picturesque lake. Virtually his entire landscape oeuvre originated here. Leaving aside these prolonged excursions, Klimt did not relish travel, became homesick after only a few days on the road, and generally was not comfortable enough away from Vienna to produce any paintings.

It is said that Klimt was fascinated by water and could spend hours just staring at the lake, watching the changing patterns of light and color. His *Island in the Attersee* (the Litzlberg Island opposite the tavern of the same name where he stayed between 1900 and 1907) is certainly suggestive of such preoccupations. Though aspects of the painting could be called Impressionistic or pointillistic, Klimt was not trying to render the effects of natural light so much as to create a tone-poem wherein multi-hued dabs of paint, tuned to a similar pitch, vibrate together in transcendent harmony. Also characteristic not only of late Impressionism but also of Art Nouveau is Klimt's high horizon line, which in this case thrusts all the compositional activity almost off the picture plane. Over ninety percent of the painting is pure surface, a delicately modulated field of brush strokes that nearly loses hold of objective reality and approaches total abstraction.

PLATE 5

PORTRAIT OF EMILIE FLÖGE

1902

Oil on canvas, 71 ¼ × 33 ⅛" (181 × 84 cm.).

Wien Museum

(N/D 126)

Even during Klimt's lifetime, it was widely assumed that he and Emilie Flöge were lovers, yet the truth of the matter, like many things concerning *fin-de-siècle* sexual mores, may be considerably more complex. Emilie Flöge, twelve years Klimt's junior, was the sister of his brother Ernst's wife. When, some fifteen months after his marriage, Ernst died, Gustav was appointed guardian of the couple's newborn daughter. In this capacity, he had free reign in the Flöge household and became something of a surrogate uncle to young Emilie. The surviving correspondence between the two is voluminous, yet entirely platonic; their "trysts" involved such innocent activities as French lessons. Would the family have tolerated Klimt's presence in their summer home on the Attersee (see plate 4), as they did almost every year, had the two been clandestine lovers? And would Klimt so openly have paraded his mistress at the theater and opera, as he did Emilie? Klimt's real lovers, as is now known, were not such nice, middle-class ladies, but models and charwomen. If Emilie was the love of his life, she was a pure and sacred love, a Madonna to the whores who, figuratively and literally, occupied the dark alleys of *fin-de-siècle* sexuality.

It is perhaps no wonder that Klimt's *Portrait of Emilie Flöge,* painted in 1902, was the first to present its subject as a bejeweled icon, a gilded beauty whose decorative trappings constitute a metaphorical chastity belt. Directly anticipating the "gold" portraits of 1906–1907 (plates 9 and 11), the picture was exceedingly radical for its day, and perhaps for this reason neither Emilie nor her family liked it. The Flöges declined to hang the painting, and in 1908 it was acquired by the City of Vienna. It was Emilie's fate also, in the end, to be rejected. In 1904, she and her sisters, Helene and Pauline, had opened a fashion salon, smartly outfitted by the Wiener Werkstätte, in Vienna's Casa Piccola. This entrepreneurial venture (unusual for women at the time) was necessitated by the financial decline of the once-prosperous Flöge family, and by the fact that the sisters, in their thirties, were too old to be considered reasonable marital prospects. Klimt, with all his avuncular affection, would not marry Emilie, preferring to retain his freewheeling bachelor's existence. Once he expressed his attitude in a whimsical poem:

> In weather fair or foul,
> Every year I tell you true:
> Rather than ever marry,
> I shall give a painting to you.

Despite Klimt's notorious philandering, Emilie remained true to him not only throughout his life, but also thereafter; she never married. Even after the Nazi *Anschluss* in 1938 forced the closing of the fashion salon, she maintained a "Klimt room" on its premises, in which stood the artist's easel and his massive cupboard, housing his collection of ornamental gowns, his caftan-like painter's smocks, and several hundred drawings. The doors of that room were always kept bolted.

PLATE 6

WATER SERPENTS I

c. 1904–1907

Mixed media on parchment, $19^{5}/_{8} \times 7^{7}/_{8}''$ (50 $\times$ 20 cm.)

Österreichische Galerie, Vienna

(N/D 139)

Klimt's *Water Serpents I* (also known by the somewhat euphemistic title *The Friends*) was the first of several images he would paint depicting lesbian relationships (see plate 22). The subject was a popular one among *fin-de-siècle* art connoisseurs, who relished the notion of women as self-sufficient hermaphrodites awash in a sea of sexual impulses. The watery surround was both perilous—a man would drown in such an environment—and elemental, representing a kind of primordial life force. Within the latter context, the women are not so much homosexual as pre-sexual. As elsewhere in Klimt's work, form is function, and the ambiguous figure-ground relationship set up by the women's stylized, almost two-dimensional bodies mirrors the ambiguity of their sexual situation. Klimt cleverly avoided the distracting spatial referrents that hampered more conventional renderings of the lesbian theme, condensing the figures within a tight column of abstract forms. Though its small size, and the fact that it is painted on parchment, suggest a very private piece of erotica, the *Water Serpents* achieves a remarkable monumentality of form.

Worked on over a period of years, the *Water Serpents* bridged the span between Klimt's earlier, pseudo-Impressionistic style (seen in his landscapes, plate 4, and such works as the *Portrait of Sonja Knips*, plate 1), and the harsher geometricity of the "gold" period. Of course, gold was hardly a new element in Klimt's repertoire: gilded architectural settings and gilded frames had always surrounded his paintings, and even in the nineteenth century he had allowed the metallic leaf to enter the canvases themselves (see plate 2). The 1902 *Portrait of Emilie Flöge* (plate 5) already contained the sort of meticulously fragmented ornamentation that, under the influence of the Ravenna mosaics, would blossom forth in the subsequent paintings of Fritza Riedler (plate 9) and Adele Bloch-Bauer (plate 11). The *horror vacui* epitomized by the densely packed surfaces of the "golden" (or "mosaic") paintings has often been interpreted as a deliberate retreat from the existential void described in prior allegories such as *Philosophy* (fig. 8) and *Medicine* (fig. 9), but in truth the void was always implicit in the decorative fill, and Klimt returned to it again and again in his work.

PLATE 7

THE THREE AGES OF WOMAN

1905

Oil on canvas, 70⁷/₈ × 70⁷/₈" (180 × 180 cm.)

Galleria Nazionale d'Arte Moderna, Rome

(N/D 141)

The Three Ages of Woman was Klimt's first large-scale private allegory, and the first to abandon entirely the use of historical or mythological symbolism. Prior to this, he had painted smaller, less complex allegories, such as *Judith I* (plate 3), for a private audience, but his bigger, multi-figure panels had always been intended for public display. *The Three Ages of Woman* thus stands halfway between earlier commissions like the University paintings (figs. 8, 9, 10) and the large allegorical canvases of the artist's last years (plates 18, 19, 24). Even the individual characters look backward as well as forward: all three women may be discerned in *Medicine* (fig. 9), while the mother and child turn up, in altered form, in *Death and Life* (plate 18). It is also significant that, as in his previous "private" allegories, Klimt concentrated his attentions exclusively on the female figure.

The painting presents its elemental message—"in life we are in death"—not only through the three principal characters, but also via a complex network of adjunct symbols. Like the *Water Serpents I* (plate 6), the women are encapsulated in a sea of baubles representative of the life force. However, now the "column of life" is isolated within a surrounding void, which, despite the touch of Klimt's decorating hand, offers a far gloomier, more barren environment than the teeming cocoon within which the protagonists rest. Death—here, as in other paintings by Klimt, represented by the color blue—awaits ominously on the horizon, winding its gossamer threads even about the legs of the innocent young mother.

PLATE 8

PORTRAIT OF MARGARET STONBOROUGH-WITTGENSTEIN

c. 1904–1905

Oil on canvas, 70 7/8 × 35 3/8″ (180 × 90 cm.)

Neue Pinakothek, Munich

(N/D 142)

Margaret Stonborough-Wittgenstein was in many ways the quintessential Klimt subject. Daughter of Karl Wittgenstein, the wealthy collector who had almost single-handedly financed the Secession's building, and sister of the philosopher Ludwig Wittgenstein and the pianist Paul Wittgenstein, she personified the mingling of money, art, and intellect at the heart of *fin-de-siècle* Vienna. Josef Hoffmann and Koloman Moser designed her Berlin apartment, Hoffmann her father's hunting lodge; her brother Ludwig, who dabbled in architecture, would build her a house in the 1920s. What then could be more natural than to commission her wedding portrait from the leading artist of the day, Gustav Klimt?

Like the *Portrait of Emilie Flöge* (plate 5), which preceded it by roughly three years, Klimt's painting of Margaret Stonborough-Wittgenstein was popular neither with the sitter nor with the artist himself, who fussed with it for months and still considered it unfinished when he first exhibited it in the autumn of 1905. (This was not unusual for Klimt, who often worked and reworked his canvases in frustration and was always reluctant to give them up; one of his clients recalled simply absconding with her portrait when, after six months, he would not relinquish it.) The problem here was different from but not unrelated to that posed by the Flöge painting. An allegorical presentation, such as *Judith I* (plate 3) or the *Water Serpents I* (plate 6), allowed Klimt's imagination full sway, whereas a portrait had to satisfy the sitter with an accurate likeness. It was apparently this very issue that irritated the Wittgensteins (who supposedly never hung the picture), for try as Klimt might to imbue Margaret with a soul, she remained something of a wax doll. Even so, the artist did not dare go so far as he had when painting his friend Emilie; he confined his use of decorative patterning to the background, and garbed the subject in a conventionally rendered gown. Margaret, in her long white dress, seems aesthetically closer to Sonja Knips (plate 1) than to Emilie Flöge. The two distinct styles used for the figure and the ground probably do not work to the sitter's advantage, for one cannot help feeling that the wallpaper is more interesting than the woman. As in Klimt's previous work, the abstract patterning has more pictorial presence—and hence is more "real"—than the naturalistically modeled figure. Even leaving aside Margaret's wounded vanity, it was not an entirely satisfactory artistic solution. At the same time, precisely because the background is given such an independent identity, the painting is often cited as one of those in which Klimt comes closest to pursuing abstraction as an end in itself.

PLATE 9

PORTRAIT OF FRITZA RIEDLER

1906

Oil on canvas, 60 1/4 × 52-3/8" (153 × 133 cm.)

Österreichische Galerie, Vienna

(N/D 143)

Within roughly one year of completing the *Portrait of Margaret Stonborough-Wittgenstein* (plate 8), Klimt found the solution he was looking for in his *Portrait of Fritza Riedler.* The similarities between the two paintings—both women wear white dresses and pose against ornamental backgrounds—only accentuate the seeming ease with which the artist suddenly resolved problems that just recently had appeared insurmountable. To do so, first of all, he had recourse to the triangular configuration that had served him so well in the *Portrait of Sonja Knips* (plate 1). By encrusting the encircling armchair with Egyptian eye motifs, Klimt established a spatial ambiguity that he deftly manipulated to his advantage. The plane that should, logically, be furthest forward assumes a recessive flatness that automatically connects with the decorative background. A similar ambiguity is created in the ovoid shape that surmounts the woman's head. Observers have long endeavored to ascribe a concrete identity to the object that produced this shape: is it a stained-glass window? A Tiffany lampshade? A wallpaper pattern? Of course, it is none of these, but a pure Klimtian invention. Already in the artist's day, critics called attention to the formal relationship between this device and the headdresses worn by Veláz-quez's Spanish Infantas in his well-known portraits. The mysterious shape in the Riedler portrait is both headdress and two-dimensional wall ornament; it is attached to both the figure and the background, and mediates between the two. Through such spatial tricks, Klimt managed to avoid the isolation of figure from ground that undermined the Stonborough-Wittgenstein portrait.

The *Portrait of Fritza Riedler* and its companion, the *Portrait of Adele Bloch-Bauer* (plate 11), with which it was repeatedly shown, may be considered the climax of what has come to be known as Klimt's "gold" period. Contemporary critics called the style "mosaic painting," a formulation that is not only more accurate (for gold figures only marginally in some of the "gold" paintings), but that is also more useful in tying together the disparate strands of the artist's development. The Secession's thrust toward the applied arts and a concomitant tendency to seek artistic applications for materials previously scorned because of their crafts associations undoubtedly encouraged the study of mosaics, and Klimt was far from the first among his peers to visit Ravenna's church of San Vitale. Despite chronic homesickness for Vienna, he made two virtually consecutive trips there in 1903, and returned duly impressed with the glorious Byzantine mosaics. The "mosaic style" suited his artistic needs perfectly, admitting the architectural element he had long been seeking while at the same time offering a formal alternative to the homogeneous "mood" Impressionism that had beguiled him without entirely converting him. Long after he had abandoned the rigid structure of the gold period proper, the spirit of the painted mosaic remained with him, and his paintings were ever after composed of little chips of color.

PLATE 10

THE SUNFLOWER

c. 1906–1907

Oil on canvas, 45 1/4 × 45 1/4" (110 × 110 cm.)

Private collection

(N/D 146)

Klimt's *Sunflower* demonstrates—perhaps more clearly than the flashy "gold" paintings—the full range of the "mosaic" style. Elimination of the slick metallic surface (which demanded a concordant response in the handling of paint) allowed the artist to exploit more fully the tactile qualities of the pigment. In its landscape incarnation, the mosaic style also revealed its affinity to the *ersatz* pointillism that had earlier intrigued Klimt, a painterly impulse that, while masked in the more austere gold pictures, was to re-emerge in his later work. *The Sunflower* is, in its way, no less a mosaic than the *Portrait of Fritza Riedler* (plate 9), but it is a far softer, more sensual painting.

As the contemporary poet Peter Altenberg observed, Klimt handled the landscape as though it were a woman. With equal accuracy, it might be said that he treated women like landscapes: both were interpreted as ornamental bodies, laid out upon a flat and airless plane. With a few exceptions such as the flowery pedestal in *The Kiss* (plate 13) (which many have compared to that in *The Sunflower*), natural elements seldom intrude in Klimt's figural work, but the two subject types are nonetheless guided by similar sensibilities. If anything, the landscapes are even more airless than the figural works (wherein a conflict between the two-dimensional setting and the three-dimensional body is unavoidable); they seem to be woven from a single swath of fabric, achieving a glorious intensity of pattern reminiscent of a quilt or a Persian carpet. *The Sunflower* is among the most portraitlike of Klimt's landscapes. Its columnar shape, rising against the void, brings to mind not just the tight coupling of *The Kiss,* but all the artist's body towers. Like the figures in *The Three Ages of Woman* (plate 7), *The Sunflower* may be taken as representing humankind's isolation in the face of death. Klimt's is an elegiac sunflower—not quite as gloomy as the specimens that Egon Schiele, his Expressionist follower, would paint, but considerably less buoyant than the robust blossoms made famous by Vincent van Gogh. Van Gogh has been credited with single-handedly introducing the sunflower fad to Vienna, and it is impossible not to consider the exhibitions of his work—at the Secession in 1903 and at the Galerie Miethke in 1906—as inspiration for Klimt's painting. For all three artists, the sun was obviously a symbol of the life force, and the flower that emulated it in name as well as in shape was a natural vessel for strong allegorical sentiment.

PLATE 11

PORTRAIT OF ADELE BLOCH-BAUER I

1907

Oil, silver, and gold on canvas, 54 ⅜ × 54 ⅜" (138 × 138 cm.).

Neue Galerie New York; This acquisition made available in part through the generosity of the heirs

of the Estates of Ferdinand and Adele Bloch-Bauer   (N/D 150)

"More *Blech* [tin] than Bloch" was one critic's response when Klimt first exhibited his *Portrait of Adele Bloch-Bauer I.* Truly, it might be argued, the artist had gone too far in literally burying his subject up to her neck in metallic ornament. The formal solutions essayed in the *Portrait of Fritza Riedler* (plate 9) were here pushed to their furthest extreme: the off-center pose is similar, but the armchair can hardly be distinguished from the decorative background, and the woman's dress has ceased to have any three-dimensional presence whatsoever. Adele Bloch-Bauer is not wearing the dress, but the painting itself; she is not a person, but a work of art. Neither before nor after did any of Klimt's portraits so completely take on the qualities of a Russian icon.

Who was the woman who inspired this epiphany of the gold style? A frustrated neurotic who suffered from debilitating headaches and would disappear for days at a time into her private world, Adele had, in the custom of her era, been prevented from seeking the education she craved and instead been forced into an arranged marriage with a wealthy industrialist, Ferdinand Bloch. Like many women in her position, she found an outlet for her frustrated ambitions by establishing a salon, which was frequented by leading writers, intellectuals, and artists—including, most naturally, Gustav Klimt. It has recently been suggested that Adele and Gustav were lovers, and that the dark-haired beauty was the secret subject of the two *Judith* paintings (plates 3, 16). Certainly the artistic relationship between the pair was a close one. Klimt made more studies for Bloch-Bauer's portrait than for almost any other, and he began doing so some four years before the oil was completed. Not content with one portrait, Adele commissioned a second one in 1912 (fig. 18), earning herself the distinction of being the only woman—other than the omnipresent Emilie Flöge (plate 5)—to be painted twice by Klimt. Like Emilie, Adele kept something of a Klimt shrine in her apartment: a room devoted to his work, which housed the two portraits and four landscapes (one painted at her country villa), as well as a framed photograph of the artist. Was the alleged affair, which Adele confided only to her physician and her personal maid, just the fantasy of a lonely woman? Or does Adele's secret hold the key to Klimt's subterranean world of illicit sexuality?

Fig. 18. *Portrait of Adele Bloch-Bauer II.* 1912. Oil on canvas, 62¾ × 47¼" (190 × 120 cm.). Restituted by the Österreichische Galerie, Vienna, in 2006 to the heirs of Ferdinand Bloch-Bauer (N/D 44)

PLATE 12

DANAE

c. 1907–1908

Oil on canvas, 30 ¼ × 32 ⅝" (77 × 83 cm.).

Private collection

(N/D 151)

Klimt was far from the first to tackle the legend of Danae, a subject long established through the work of such artists as Titian. The tale concerns a creature of striking beauty, imprisoned in a tower by her father in order to preserve her virginity and thereby evade fulfillment of a deadly prophecy. The god Zeus, immune to such subterfuge, sees the fair lady in her barren lair and visits her in the form of a golden shower, thereby impregnating her and releasing her to her tragic destiny. Klimt fashioned from this myth an image embodying the inexorability of sexual desire. His *Danae* lies in a swoon, patently oblivious to her charms, yet nonetheless ruled by them. The embryonic pose thrusts her reproductive organs to the foreground; Klimt supposedly commented that one of his models had buttocks more beautiful and intelligent than most people's faces, and *Danae* would seem to illustrate the point. The symbolic shower of gold is here interpreted in the spermatozoalike forms already familiar from such paintings as *Water Serpents I* (plate 6). Like the water serpents, Danae seems to exist within a liquid ambient representing both life and death; in her womblike cocoon, she is the product as well as the victim of her sexual nature.

In paintings such as *Danae* (or, earlier, *Judith I,* plate 3), Klimt created potent, multivalent images personifying *fin-de-siècle* sexual attitudes. It is therefore not surprising that these canvases aroused little opposition from the Viennese public, which felt far less challenged by them than by the comparatively ponderous allegories, such as the University paintings (figs. 8, 9, 10). Today, attitudes are somewhat reversed, and while many of Klimt's allegories appear tame and dated, his erotic images — with their tacit acceptance of female inferiority and implicit fear of sexuality — at first glance seem rather shocking. Nevertheless, the latter remain among the artist's most compelling and enduring works. More concise than the elaborate allegories, they are able at the same time to encompass extremely complex levels of meaning; they are at once seductive and terrifying, beautiful and horrific. There was in Klimt already much of the same fascination with the morbid, forbidden, and libidinous that would find its ultimate outlet in the work of the younger Expressionist generation.

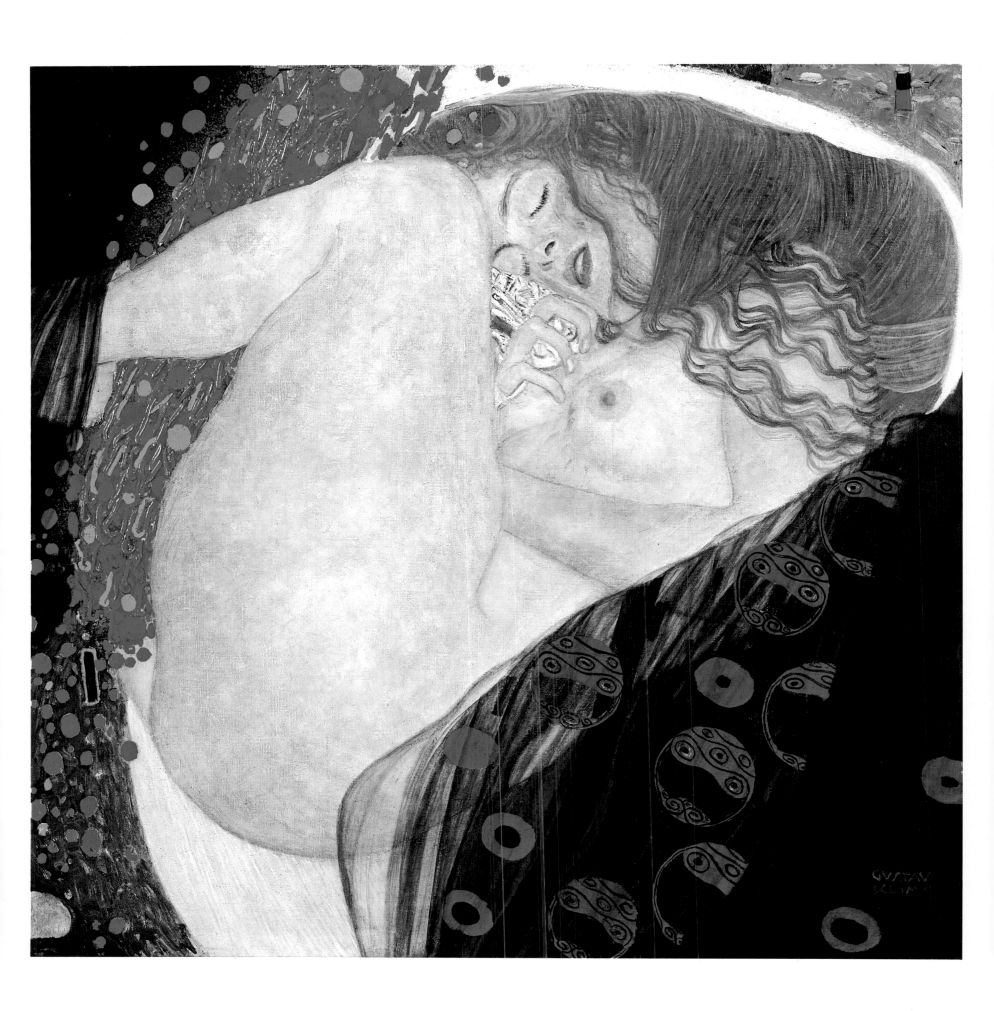

PLATE 13

THE KISS

1907–1908

Oil on canvas, 70 7/8 × 70 7/8" (180 × 180 cm.)

Österreichische Galerie, Vienna

(N/D 154)

The Kiss is surely Klimt's most popular painting, and was even in his day; prior to its completion, it had already been purchased by the Austrian state. Arguably, it is also one of his best paintings, although it lacks the complexity and depth of his more intricate allegories. It is precisely because *The Kiss* is not burdened by the weight of a ponderous philosophy, nor tied to a tradition of allegorical symbolism that has today lost much of its former meaning, that the painting remains one of Klimt's most transcendent images. The tower of bodies that recurs throughout the artist's oeuvre is here resolved into a single organic unit, a union of male and female whose meaning is clear for all to see and is so inextricably bound to its pictorial form that the whole becomes a totemic monument to love.

The love portrayed in *The Kiss* is of a very different order from the dark passion of Klimt's *Judith I* (plate 3) or even the dream ecstacy of *Danae* (plate 12). The basic incarnation of the composition can be traced to the 1902 Beethoven Frieze, where it was backed up by an extensive sequence of allegorical antecedents that provided an almost literary explanation of the artist's intentions. The Beethoven Frieze depicts man's triumph over evil—personified by an appropriate cast of females, including three gorgons (typical Klimtian *femmes fatales*) and a giantess (fig. 11)—to achieve a pure and joyous love, encapsulated in the final panel, *A Kiss for the Entire World* (fig. 12). *The Kiss* is essentially a reworking of this image, but the lack of allegorical prelude focuses all attention on the triumph and ignores the darker forces that play so important a role in the frieze, as well as in the related 1895 canvas, *Love* (fig. 4). Although the sinister potentialities of sex are not shown in *The Kiss,* they are nonetheless intrinsic to its meaning.

Careful study of the preliminary drawings for *The Kiss* has led to the hypothesis that Klimt himself posed for the painting, together with his friend Emilie Flöge (plate 5). Even in these studies (as, in fact, in most of Klimt's drawings), however, the faces are stylized, and the man, though bearded like Klimt, cannot properly be called a self-portrait. ("There exists no self-portrait by me," Klimt wrote. "I am not interested in myself as 'subject matter for a picture.'") In the final canvas—and in both the prior and subsequent (*Fulfillment,* cover) variations on the theme—Klimt concealed the man's face entirely. As with the *Portrait of Adele Bloch-Bauer I* (plate 11), it is tempting to speculate on the degree to which this painting truly reflects the artist's relationship with its female protagonist. If Bloch-Bauer represents an illicit romance, surely Flöge—whose "affair" with Klimt may never have been consummated—must represent a purer, more platonic sort of love. In the parlance of the turn-of-the-century, a woman was either a Madonna or a whore, and *The Kiss,* for all its erotic subtext, may well be an ironic icon to chastity.

PLATE 14

HOPE II

1907–1908

Oil on canvas, 43 ¹/₄ × 43 ¹/₄" (110 × 110 cm.)

The Museum of Modern Art, New York

(N/D 155)

Klimt had first felt compelled to feature a pregnant woman as the subject of a painting in 1903, possibly by the birth, and subsequent death, of one of his own illegitimate sons. He and his lover at the time, Marie Zimmermann, may have posed for the preliminary studies, but the final painting, *Hope I* (fig. 19), was an allegorical statement that intentionally breached any personal associations. The subject, while certainly not unique to Klimt, was somewhat unorthodox, and it is said that rumors flew about Vienna when the artist invited the pregnant model to his studio. *Hope I,* showing the woman's bare, bulging belly, was considered so outrageous that Klimt was dissuaded for many years from exhibiting it, and its first owner, the Wiener Werkstätte financier Fritz Waerndorfer, kept it behind specially constructed doors to shield it from the unenlightened.

 Hope II, Klimt's second focused exploration of the theme (pregnant women had appeared as subordinate images in several of his earlier allegories), was in many ways less overtly provocative than *Hope I.* The woman's abdomen was no longer bared, and the ghoulish spectres that featured so prominently in the earlier painting were here discreetly hidden in the decorative folds of her gown. Unlike *Hope I,* with its characteristic balance of detailed naturalism and ornamental encrustation, *Hope II* had weathered the full brunt of Klimt's mosaic phase and began to point, albeit tentatively, toward a different future. Many aspects of the composition were by now familiar: once again, a central pillar of bodies cut through a square canvas, and the surrounding space, however luminous in its ornamental veneer, was a negative as well as a positive area, a void as well as a presence. The somnolent stance of the principal character and her supportive sisters anticipated the dreaming heroines of Klimt's later allegories, *The Virgin* (plate 19) and *The Bride* (plate 24). Pregnancy (alluded to by such recurrent titles as "Hope" or "Expectation") was the ideal condition for the Klimtian woman, a state of physical as well as psychological waiting, of utmost passivity. In his slightly later Stoclet Frieze, the artist would pair *Expectation* (fig. 13) with its natural complement, *Fulfillment* (cover), and it is possible that a similar relationship was intended between *Hope II* and *The Kiss* (plate 13).

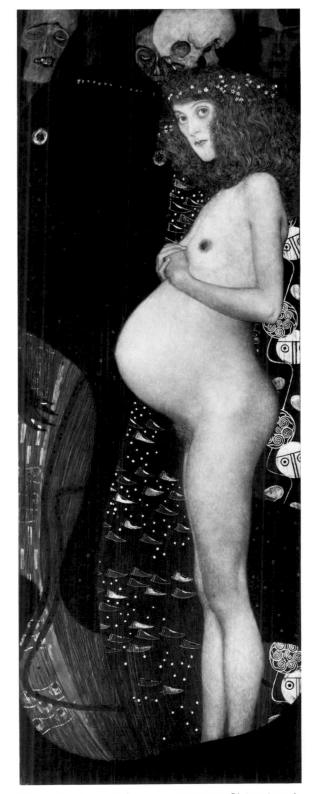

Fig. 19. *Hope I.* 1903. Oil on canvas, 71 ¹/₄ × 26 ³/₈" (181 × 67 cm.). National Gallery of Canada, Ottawa (N/D 129)

PLATE 15

SCHLOSS KAMMER ON THE ATTERSEE I

c. 1908

Oil on canvas, 43 1/4 × 43 1/4" (110 × 110 cm.)

Národní Galerie, Prague

(N/D 159)

Given that the dramatic contrast between water and surrounding mountains is the most salient characteristic of the Salzkammergut landscape, it is curious that Klimt never painted such scenes, and for the most part he favored the relatively flat, verdant area at the northern end of the Attersee over the rocky southern tip. The parklike setting of Schloss Kammer, located near the little town where he spent the summers of 1908–12, appealed to him, and he had painted the gardens surrounding the eighteenth-century villa as early as 1899. When, in 1908, he first turned his attention to the building itself, his approach remained typically static: differences of plane and texture were minimized, and the mirroring properties of the water were exaggerated to present land and lake as an unbroken continuum. Nevertheless, the introduction of an architectural element constituted a new direction, and one that was to become increasingly evident in his later work. A building-block sensibility suggestive of a cubist influence can be detected in some of the subsequent townscapes, but it is likely that Klimt originally turned to architecture simply to break the grip of overall patterning so characteristic of the mosaic style at its zenith.

Like many of his Attersee landscapes, *Schloss Kammer* was probably painted from the water. Klimt was a keen sailor and is said to have been among the first on the lake to own a motorboat. He often worked outdoors, hiding his materials in the underbrush so as not to have to drag them out each day. A photographic perspective was achieved through the use of a telescope or binoculars and a square ivory framing device. (Not coincidentally, all the artist's landscapes after 1899 were square.) Klimt did not make full-sized preliminary studies for his landscapes, and since he had come to the genre relatively late in his professional life, he was not prejudiced by the traditional training that conditioned his figural assignments. Thus these paintings often have an immediacy that is lacking in his studio work.

PLATE 16

JUDITH II (SALOME)

1909

Oil on canvas, 70 ⅛ × 18 ⅛" (178 × 46 cm.)

Galleria d'Arte Moderna, Venice

(N/D 160)

While Klimt's first *Judith* (plate 3) was erroneously called "Salome" from the start (despite the fact that the correct title was clearly embossed on the frame), *Judith II* only acquired this alternative title after Klimt's death. Careful analysis of the preliminary drawings suggests that *Salome* may actually be the more accurate designation for the latter image, which metamorphosed from studies of a dancing woman—an activity that is part of Salome's legend, but not Judith's. Other artists—notably Gustave Moreau and Aubrey Beardsley—had already made of Salome a popular *fin-de-siècle* icon, and Klimt's conception was probably also influenced by Richard Strauss's opera (based, in turn, on the 1893 play by Oscar Wilde), which had its Viennese premiere in 1907. The difference between the two legends is not without significance, for while Judith was a heroine who used her feminine wiles to seduce the enemy and then slew him, Salome (particularly as portrayed by Strauss and Wilde) was a spoiled nymphet who charmed King Herod into giving her the head of John the Baptist as a child might wheedle a coveted toy from an indulgent parent. There is no question that *Judith II,* with her claws bared and seemingly set to pounce, is a far more evil woman than *Judith I.* She is also the same dark-haired type whom Felix Salten recognized as a typical Jewish socialite, and whom one modern-day observer has identified as Adele Bloch-Bauer (plate 11). Whether *Judith II* is the testament of a love affair gone sour, or simply another incarnation of Klimt's "Jewish" *femme fatale* is a matter of debate.

Stylistically, *Judith II* falls on the waning side of Klimt's gold or mosaic period. The ornamentation is more painterly, the gilding less predominant than formerly. The attenuated vertical composition (constituting a break from the squarish format that Klimt generally favored) results in an unusually dense clustering of large and small shapes. As elsewhere, Klimt's formal innovations relate directly to the content of the work, and this packed piling-up of schematic elements is one of the things that give *Judith* her oppressive intensity. The extremity of the vertical approach here brings to mind oriental scrolls and Japanese pillar prints, or *Oban.* This was by no means the first time an oriental influence could be detected in Klimt's art (he had probably been collecting scrolls and ceremonial kimonos since the 1900 Japanese exhibition at the Secession), but it did herald a more conscious awareness of such art forms. Japanese motifs were to play a dominant role in his later work.

PLATE 17

APPLE TREE I

c. 1912

Oil on canvas, 43 ¼ × 43 ¼" (110 × 110 cm.).

Restituted by the Österreichische Galerie, Vienna, in

2006 to the heirs of Ferdinand Bloch-Bauer (N/D 151)

At first glance Klimt's landscapes would seem to show a smoother line of development than his figural works. While they evidence a parallel transition from silky pseudo-Impressionism to the more crystalline painted mosaic style, the latter phase is not distinguished by the rigid geometricity and harsh metallic colors found in the portraits and allegories. Klimt's passage into his last, most painterly period thus also transpired more organically in the landscapes, for the landscapes had never altogether succumbed to the linearity of the middle stage. In fact, it may be said that landscape was the wellspring from which much of his revitalized later art sprang, and even his portraits benefited from spatial devices perfected in this genre (plates 20, 21).

Klimt was a master of tricks that simultaneously created and destroyed the illusion of depth, and in a painting such as *Apple Tree I,* one can logically distinguish at least four distinct planes: the larger flowers in the foreground, the field between them and the tree, the tree itself, and the lush foliage beyond. Yet the overall pattern of brushstroke insistently informs us that this is a sham, the painting is as flat as the canvas that supports it. Such deliberate manipulation of the picture plane catered to the abstractionist tendencies that had always been inherent in Klimt's approach to landscape. Indeed, whereas in his portraits convention (not to mention the sitter's vanity) demanded a persistent loyalty to volumetric verisimilitude, Klimt in his landscapes was freer both in his manner of seeing and in his ultimate goals. The landscapes (with no one to please but Klimt himself) are the most purely *artistic* works in his oeuvre, evidencing a painter's delight in form, color, and texture for their own sakes. Particularly in his more abstract late landscapes, Klimt achieved a unity of conception that brings these works, like the last landscapes of Monet, to the very forefront of Modernism.

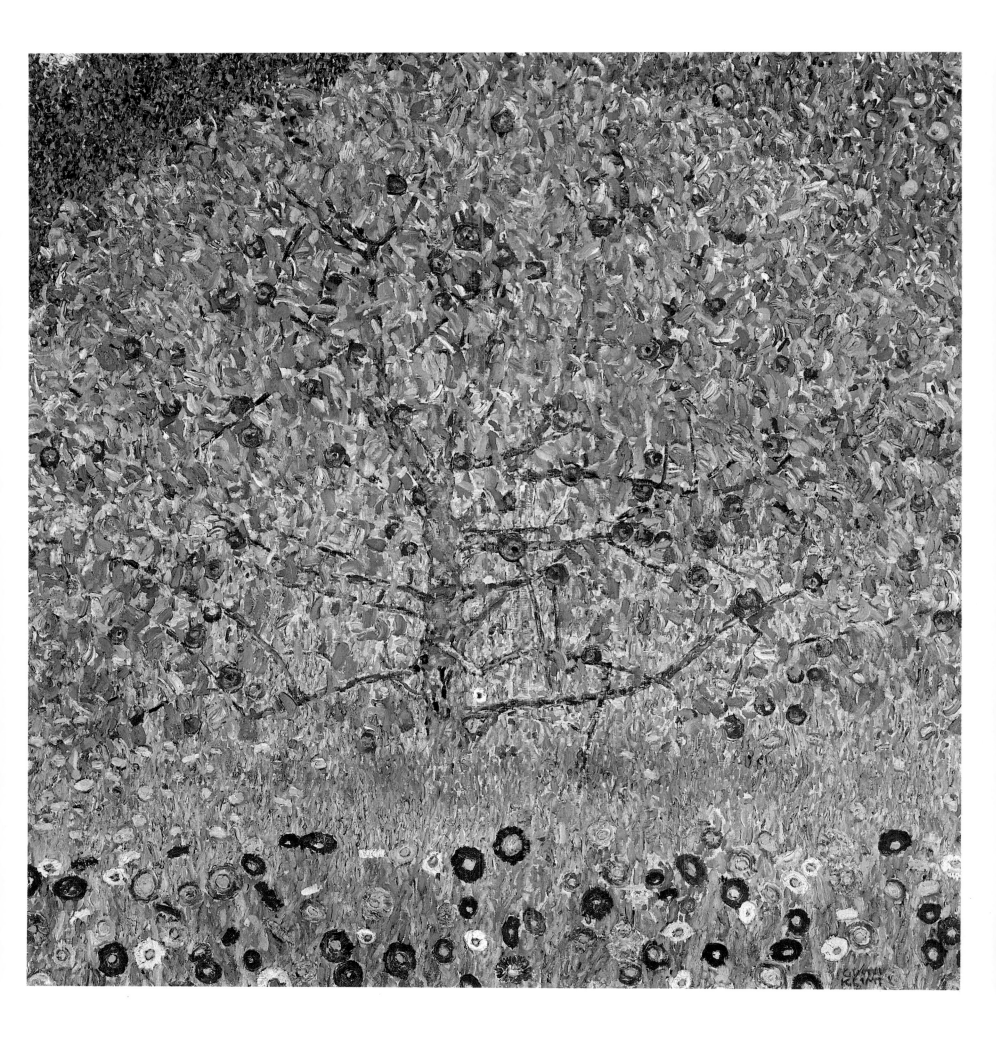

PLATE 18

DEATH AND LIFE

1908–11; revised 1915–16

Oil on canvas, 70 ⅛ × 78" (178 × 198 cm.).

Leopold Museum, Vienna

(N/D 183)

In *Death and Life,* Klimt returned to a theme that had interested him since the University paintings: that of the mass of humanity confronting the uncertainty of existence and the certainty of death. The theme is specifically closest to *Medicine* (fig. 9), though a similar idea is explored in *Philosophy* (fig. 8) and *The Three Ages of Woman* (plate 7). The "tower of humanity" that had by now become something of a Klimt trademark (and that viewers found so distressing when they first saw it in *Philosophy*) can be traced back to a quite conventional Ringstrasse mural by Hans Canon and, perhaps more significantly, to a well-known Viennese landmark: the so-called *Pestsäule* (Plague Column) that stands in the heart of the city as a monument to the Great Plague. The pervasive presence of death in life commemorated by the Baroque *Pestsäule* was the subterranean current that gave Klimt's art its elusive power, belying the glittery surfaces that have prompted some to dismiss him as a mere decorator. This subliminal pessimism was also his most enduring legacy to the Expressionist generation, in particular Egon Schiele.

The contrast between morbidity and dazzle in Klimt's work has seldom been sharper than in *Death and Life,* as is evident from the conflicting interpretations the painting has spawned. The canvas, which may have been begun as early as 1908, originally had a gold background, and the death's head, surmounted by a halo, was sunken into the figure's cloak. By bringing forward the grinning skull, removing the halo (a symbolic reference to reincarnation), and overpainting the background with blue (always, for Klimt, the color of death), the artist considerably strengthened the fearful undertones of the painting in its final version. On the other hand, the sugary sweetness of his palette and the deliberate separation of "Death" from "Life" seems to yield a weaker, more optimistic portrayal of the theme than earlier formulations such as *Medicine,* which depicted death as an integral part of life. Indeed, the key to the interpretation depends on how one perceives the background void (which already in *The Three Ages of Woman* had begun to figure prominently in Klimt's allegories). Only if one understands the symbolism behind the blue coloring does one see that the column of life is, in fact, wholly engulfed in death.

PLATE 19

THE VIRGIN

1912–13

Oil on canvas, 74³/₄ × 78³/₄″ (190 × 200 cm.)

Národní Galerie, Prague

(N/D 184)

The Virgin may be considered the first of Klimt's late allegories (*Death and Life,* plate 18, though begun earlier, was finished later). Like many of the artist's paintings, *The Virgin* presents its theme as a mass of humanity, set within an encompassing void. The oval contours of the mass, and the virgin's somnolent state, recall the earlier *Danae* (plate 12), while the pose anticipates *The Bride* (plate 24). The bright palette, with its predominance of pastels, and the softer, more painterly approach, connect the painting with Klimt's later period, but the ornamentation, particularly of the virgin's dress, still has the oppressive, inorganic quality of the mosaic style. Thematically, *The Virgin* expounds upon the same state of passive anticipation essayed in *Expectation* (fig. 13) and *Hope II* (plate 14), while also foreshadowing *The Bride.* It is thus in many ways a transitional work.

After completing the Stoclet Frieze in 1910 (cover, figs. 13, 14), Klimt received no more allegorical commissions. The problems of that last assignment may well have convinced him that the purposes of art and architecture were inimical to one another, but he was not about to give up the tradition of symbolism that had been the mainstay of the Ringstrasse era and his own *raison d'être* from the very start of his career. It is a curious fact that later allegories such as *The Virgin* served no logical purpose or market; they were, on the whole, rather difficult to sell. Klimt's persistence in this not very lucrative vein attests to his enduring belief that art must serve some higher spiritual purpose; it was a lesson not lost on his protégé, Egon Schiele, who also painted many unsalable allegories. Klimt, for his part, was not entirely uninfluenced by the younger artist, and the personal symbolism of his last allegories, though not always wholly successful, attests to his desire to expand beyond the historical and mythological framework of his earlier style. If the looser brushwork of his late paintings was more Expressionistic in style than in substance, it nonetheless bespoke a desire to adapt to the changing creative environment. Few artists have manifested the potential for continued growth that Klimt did in the final years of his life.

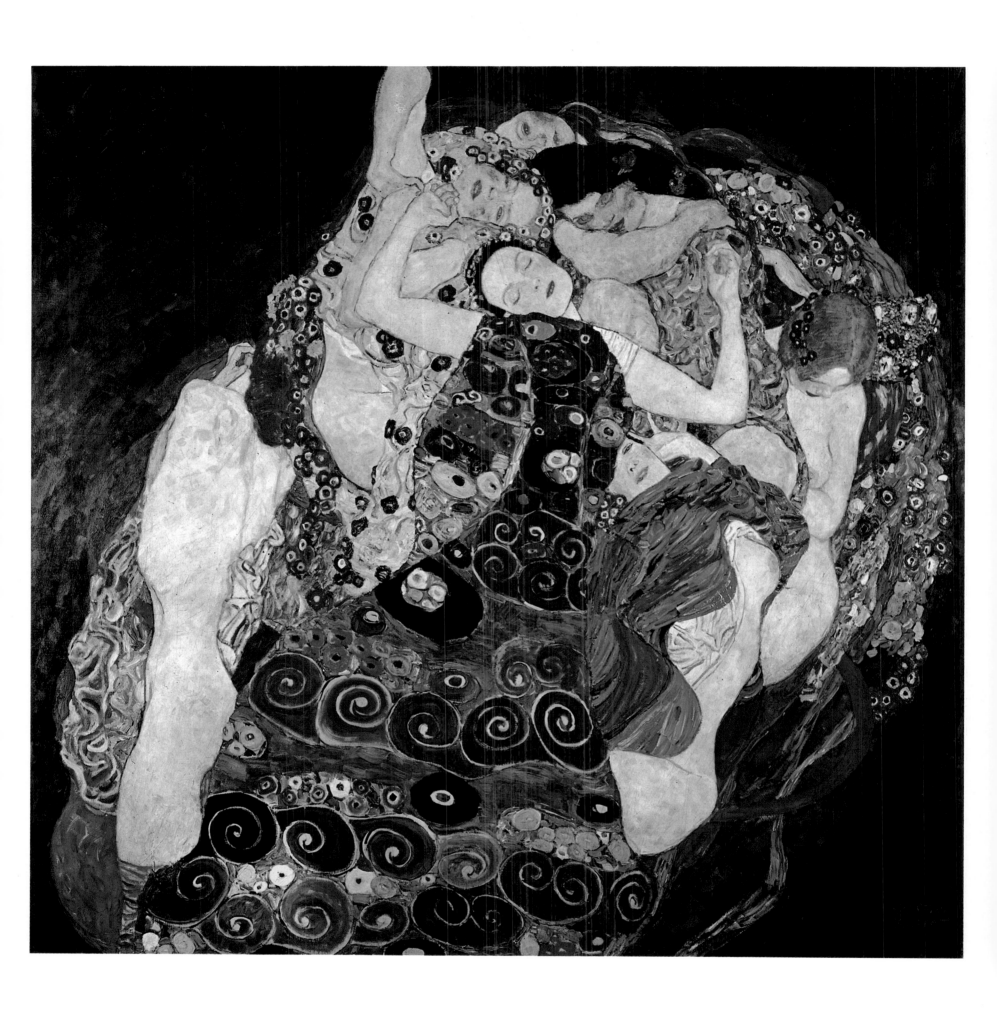

PLATE 20

PORTRAIT OF MÄDA PRIMAVESI

c. 1912–13

Oil on canvas, 59 × 43¼" (150 × 110 cm.)

The Metropolitan Museum of Art, New York

(N/D 179)

Mäda Primavesi was a child who had everything: the daughter of Otto Primavesi, one of the Wiener Werkstätte's principal backers, she lived a fairy-tale existence in her parents' remote Moravian villa, designed in lavish Werkstätte fashion by the redoubtable Josef Hoffmann. Klimt's portrait, with its sugary pinks and whites, is both an accurate reflection of the subject's charmed life and a sympathetic portrait of a very real (and somewhat willful) little girl. Klimt had an instinctive understanding of children, though he rarely had the opportunity to paint them. Mäda remembered him as a kindly fellow, who seemed to understand the ten-year-old's desire to move about and did not insist (as had a "conventional" painter for whom she sat years earlier) that she remain absolutely still. Others have noted that Klimt was himself rather childlike; he enjoyed throwing paper hats from the window of the Flöge fashion salon and watching them alight on the heads of unsuspecting strangers below.

Like Klimt's earlier portraits, this one pits its subject against a decorative background, but the inherent conflict between the two-dimensional and the three-dimensional has been softened by a more painterly application of pigment. Mäda is not trapped in the paint surface (as were Klimt's gilded icons); she blends organically into it. Furthermore, the space in which she stands is not quite so airless as that in the mosaic portraits. The setting might almost be a landscape, and, indeed, the pink backdrop could be read as either a wall or the sky; the flowers on the putative "horizon" might be real or part of a carpet pattern. The white triangular surface upon which the child stands, like the foreshortened paths in some of the artist's landscapes, suggests spatial depth while remaining manifestly two-dimensional. (A similar device would later be used in the *Portrait of the Baroness Elisabeth Bachofen-Echt,* plate 21.) Echoed by Mäda's stance, this triangular shape strikes an intriguing balance between foreground and background, focusing attention very sharply on the subject. The Primavesi picture is in many ways a more accomplished painting and a more successful portrait than much of the artist's earlier work.

PLATE 21

PORTRAIT OF THE BARONESS ELISABETH BACHOFEN-ECHT

c. 1914–16

Oil on canvas, 70⅞ × 50⅜" (180 × 128 cm.)

Private collection

(N/D 188)

Elisabeth Bachofen-Echt (née Lederer) was the daughter of August and Serena Lederer, Klimt's most important patrons. The family's collection eventually grew to include some fifteen canvases by the artist, among them an 1899 portrait of Serena—described by those who knew her as the best-dressed woman in Vienna—and a 1915 painting of her mother, Charlotte Pulitzer, a relation of Joseph Pulitzer, founder of the famous prize for writing. Elisabeth was twenty years old in 1914, when Klimt began the preparatory studies for the portrait he would complete some two years later. As in the Primavesi painting (plate 20) and, indeed, in almost all his late portraits, he chose a standing pose and used a "horizon-line" approach to divide the background into two planes. In the Bachofen-Echt portrait, the line of demarcation is lower, so that the illusion of a landscape setting is diminished, though as in Klimt's landscapes, the horizontal and vertical planes can easily be read as two perfectly flat bands of color. Elisabeth's stance is echoed by a triangular configuration similar to that in the Primavesi painting, but this shape is here placed against the back wall rather than on the floor, so that any feeling of perspectival distance it may create is automatically cut short, snapped back to the foreground by the woman's face, which forms the triangle's apex. Like the Primavesi portrait, this one amply evidences the artist's ability to manipulate space in order to enhance his sitter's presence.

The use of concrete oriental motifs—which were to become increasingly pronounced in Klimt's subsequent work—was an important innovation in the Bachofen-Echt picture. The influence of the Orient in compositions such as *Judith II* (plate 16) has already been noted. What distinguishes the later work is the extraction of isolated pictorial elements and their adaptation to Klimt's own idiosyncratic ends. Just as in the 1916 *Portrait of Friederike Maria Beer* (fig. 15) Klimt would use figures from a Korean vase for the background, he here fashioned Elisabeth's triangular "veil" on the pattern of a traditional Chinese dragon robe. Elisabeth's exotic outfit, however, is not an invention of Klimt's. Such harem ensembles, popularized by the stage designer Leon Bakst, had become the rage at the Wiener Werkstätte, and Elisabeth (like her mother) naturally dressed in the height of fashion. (A harem outfit was also worn by Friederike Maria Beer for her portrait.)

PLATE 22

THE FRIENDS

c. 1916–17

Oil on canvas, 39 × 39″ (99 × 99 cm.)(?)

Destroyed

(N/D 201)

Klimt's appropriation of oriental ornamentation reached its high point around 1917 with such paintings as *The Friends*. Of course, iconographical borrowing, the mainstay of his earliest commissions, was not new to the artist, nor was he a stranger to Japanese design. Throughout the mosaic period he had explored ambiguous figure/ground relationships similar to those seen in Japanese prints, but his nagging fidelity to three-dimensional verisimilitude had always prevented him from achieving total planar unity. In the end, he found his solution not in the linearity of the Japanese approach (and of his own gold paintings), but rather in a return to lusher, more densely impastoed surfaces. The orange robe, pink wallpaper and rosy flesh of *The Friends* are all handled with the same buttery strokes, and by this means, the background motifs acquire a pictorial presence that makes them as "real" as the main subjects. It is impossible to determine whether the women and their feathered companions occupy the same plane or not. Background becomes foreground and, as a result, foreground background. Like so much of Klimt's late work, the painting is partially about space and the various illusions that art creates to deal with it.

Thematically, of course, the subject of *The Friends* was a recapitulation of the lesbian imagery that had recurred in Klimt's work ever since the 1904 *Water Serpents I* (plate 6). However, the world in which *The Friends* dwell seems a much less forbidding place than that of the *Water Serpents,* and they much less forbidding people. Despite the surreal spatial qualities of the canvas, it is evident that this couple does not inhabit the watery depths, but lives above ground, breathing real air. Both faces are shown, and they engage the viewer sympathetically. The feeling between them is less erotic passion than tender affection, and the "unnatural" homosexual union is here given a yin/yang quality of inevitability. This dualism is expressed both by the physical appearances of the two—one clothed and one naked—and by the birds that flank them. On the left is a fantastic phoenix, symbol of regeneration, while on the right are the inevitable forces of doom, the raven and the evil, red-eyed swan. The friends thus become symbols of the eternal human predicament, a couple whose situation, far from being anomalous, assumes a prototypical magnitude.

PLATE 23

ADAM AND EVE

1917

Oil on canvas, 68 1/8 × 23 5/8" (173 × 60 cm.)

Österreichische Galerie, Vienna

(N/D 220)

If one excepts the apocryphal story of Judith and Holofernes and the related Salome (see plates 3, 16), *Adam and Eve* was Klimt's first biblical painting. Certainly it was the only one to present humankind in a state of grace, for the scene would seem to be set before the Fall, perhaps at the moment of Eve's creation. As the sole truly chaste woman, Eve is a heroine very different from Judith, or indeed from any of the artist's *femmes fatales.* Klimt's contemporaries remarked that his ideal woman generally departed significantly from the Viennese notion of beauty: she was slender rather than buxom, redhaired or brunette rather than blond. This "Old Testament type" (as Klimt's typical heroine was euphemistically called) had an aura of exoticism that was both appealing and intentionally frightening. A sword that cut both ways, his conception of the *femme fatale* indulged latent anti-Semitic fears while at the same time glorifying the very subject of those fears. It is not surprising that, for this reason (and because many of his patrons were Jewish), Klimt was subject to anti-Semitic attacks. Be that as it may, it is curious to note that when he chose his model for the mother of the human race, he picked a blond, "pure-blooded Aryan" type—one of the few to appear in his paintings.

There are other aspects of *Adam and Eve* that distinguish it from the rest of Klimt's oeuvre. Thematically, it was an extension of the many versions of "The Kiss" (cover, plate 13, fig. 12), and the preliminary drawings indicate that the composition evolved directly from these earlier works. However, whereas in all the incarnations of "The Kiss" the man dominates, here it is Eve who is pushed to the forefront. Studies suggest that Klimt considered posing her with her back turned (like the man in the "Kisses"), but decided to position both figures facing forward so that their faces could be seen (another departure from the prior works). As a result, Adam has more presence than most of Klimt's male characters, though his role is hardly a strong one. In a curious reversal of the usual symbolism, the man is passive, somnolent, while the woman is active, awake. Night (or the moon) was traditionally the female force, day (the sun) male, and they were thus portrayed in the Beethoven Frieze version of "The Kiss" (fig. 12). Here, however, it is the man who seems associated with night, while the lighter female radiates sunshine. Klimt was gradually breaking out of the *fin-de-siècle* stereotypes of sexuality to embrace a broader and more original vision.

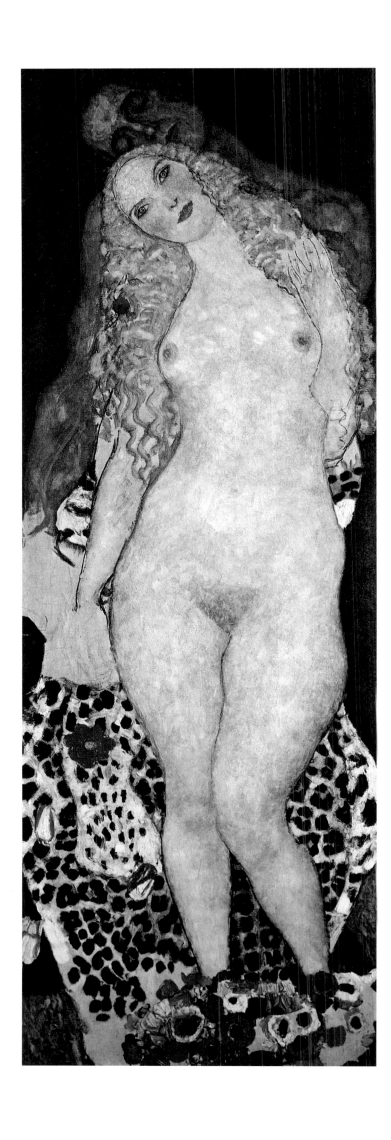

PLATE 24

THE BRIDE

1917–18

Oil on canvas, 65 3/8 × 74 3/4" (166 × 190 cm.)

Private collection

(N/D 222)

The Bride, like *Adam and Eve* (plate 23), was one of the canvases left unfinished at the time of Klimt's death in 1918. It is surprising that a work so unresolved, and therefore ambiguous, has nonetheless generally been considered a major component of his artistic legacy. It is, perhaps, the very ambiguity, the penetrating mystery of the painting that accounts for its enduring appeal. Then, too, *The Bride* has the fascination of a work-in-progress, allowing an intimate glimpse of the creative mechanism. The *pentimenti* reveal, more clearly than any of his finished canvases, Klimt's strategy of working from the nude and then "clothing" his figures in paint. This process allowed the artist to distance the artificial, painterly world of his canvases from that of his flesh-and-blood models by using drawing as a two-dimensional intermediary. Clearly, many details of his pictures were only worked out in the act of painting, and this explains why he created few full-fledged compositional studies for his oils and did not usually color his drawings.

But *The Bride* keeps more secrets than it reveals. The column of life on the left—by now a familiar device—is the most finished aspect of the painting. Would it eventually have been joined by a similar structure on the right? One cannot be sure, though it is clear that the recumbent woman on that side of the canvas would not have been alone. And what, then, of the solitary figure in the middle, the bride herself? Positioned between the two clusters of humanity, she fills the hollow void that had, in all Klimt's other late allegories, come to play an important symbolic role. Her face, possibly based on a Noh mask, is a complete blank; she derives her identity from the forces around her, much as the Japanese actor submerges his personality in the formal apparatus of his costume to assume a totemic function. But just what is her relationship to these surrounding forces? Are the body bundles, as one writer has suggested, her dream visions? Do they, as another has hypothesized, represent two bacchantic visions of femininity? Or do they, like *Adam and Eve,* embody two alternative responses to life, an active and a passive? Klimt's symbolism had become increasingly personal and decreasingly literary ever since the University debacle, and it is impossible to know whether *The Bride* would have eventually resolved itself into some generally understandable statement. It is tempting to imagine that in his final painting Klimt might at last have found a vehicle for allegory that, by creating a surreal world of pure form and color, transcended conventional notions of both subject and space. Unfortunately, we will never know if *The Bride* heralds such a triumph, for this, like the other enigmas of Klimt's life, went with him to the grave.

CARTOON FOR THE STOCLET FRIEZE: FULFILLMENT

c. 1908–10

Mixed media on paper, 76⅜ × 47⅝″ (194 × 121 cm.)

Österreichisches Museum für angewandte Kunst, Vienna

(N/D 152-1)

Fulfillment, the last of Klimt's three monumental versions of *The Kiss* (plate 13), was, like that in the Beethoven Frieze (fig. 12), part of a larger mural. Commissioned by the Wiener Werkstätte around 1906 and executed by the mosaic workshop of Leopold Forstner between 1910 and 1911, it was ultimately installed in the dining room of Adolphe Stoclet's lavish Brussels mansion (fig. 14). The Palais Stoclet, designed by the Wiener Werkstätte down to the last teaspoon, was the epitome of the *Gesamtkunstwerk* (total artwork) as interpreted by that organization, and the commission satisfied Klimt's longstanding desire to merge art and reality by reconciling architecture with pictorial illusion. What better assignment could there be for someone who painted in a "mosaic style" than to design an actual mosaic? The Wiener Werkstätte gave him the opportunity to work with real materials—not just mosaics, but metal, enamel, and glass—that he had heretofore mimicked in his paintings.

In the event, however, the Stoclet Frieze proved more challenging than rewarding, as Klimt fussed and fumed over the full-sized cartoons, delaying his departure for the Attersee so that he could at last be done with the project, which he likened to "an abscess on my neck." When finally he decided to bring the paintings with him to the country, matters did not improve, and legend has it that once Emilie Flöge (plate 5) took up the brush and began to fill in the blank shapes. When Klimt saw what she was up to, he only nodded and said, "That's good. Keep going. You do it better than I." The final cartoons contain detailed instructions on how they should be interpreted in mosaic, and Klimt supervised Forstner's work closely, making adjustments along the way to accommodate the requirements of the unfamiliar medium. It was a frustrating process, and in the end Klimt still believed there were things that could have been done better, or that he would have done differently, had he to do it over again. Do it over again he would not, for when Josef Hoffmann, the Werkstätte's director, offered him a second, similar project, Klimt turned him down in no uncertain terms. "I work too ponderously," he wrote. "Stoklet [*sic*] comes naturally neither from my head nor my hand." Klimt's first real mosaic was also his last, and in rejecting the idea, he also renounced, gradually, the more salient aspects of his mosaic (or "golden") style.

Klimt was too harsh on himself if he considered the Stoclet Frieze a failure, but he was correct in perceiving that the inherent conflict between art and interior decoration made any future such ventures pointless. As a picture with a story to tell, the Stoclet Frieze is far simpler than the Beethoven mural. There are no "evil powers" here (unless one considers the intermittent black ravens to be portents of doom); nothing that might unduly disturb M. Stoclet's dinner guests. Instead of the battle of life essayed in the Beethoven Frieze, there is an all-embracing "Tree of Life," and life's struggles are reduced to *Expectation* (fig. 13) and *Fulfillment,* as though the latter were the natural outcome of the former, rather than a hard-won reward. Taking into account the inflexible materials for which he was designing, Klimt subordinated his principal figures to a sweeping geometric pattern. When the single panel *Fulfillment* is reproduced alone (as it most often is), one does not realize the extent to which the actual installation is dominated by the spiraling tree. This overwhelming concern with pattern led to Klimt's only wholly abstract work, the panel designed for the short back wall of the dining room (fig. 14). From the point of view of later modernism, Klimt's greatest failing—and that of his Viennese colleagues—was the inability to free abstraction from its architectural origins and endow it with an aesthetic or spiritual life of its own.